MICHEL QUOIST

Meeting God

Translated by N. D. Smith

Gill and Macmillan
Dimension Books

Published in Ireland by
Gill and Macmillan Ltd
Goldenbridge
Dublin 8
with associated companies in
Auckland, Delhi, Gaborone, Hamburg, Harare,
Hong Kong, Johannesburg, Kuala Lumpur, Lagos, London,
Manzini, Melbourne, Mexico City, Nairobi,
New York, Singapore, Tokyo
© Michel Quoist 1985
Translation © Gill and Macmillan 1985
Second impression 1989
0 7171 1412 0
Excerpts from *The Jerusalem Bible,*
published and copyright © 1966, 1967, 1968 Darton, Longman & Todd Ltd
and Doubleday & Company Inc.
are used by permission of the publishers.
Print origination in Ireland by
M & J Graphics Limited, Dublin
Printed in Hong Kong

First published in the United States of America
by Dimension Books Inc.,
P.O. Box 811, Denville, New Jersey 07834.
ISBN 0-87193-222-9

Contents

Introduction

These meditations are homilies I have preached in various parishes in France before the television cameras. In other words, they were addressed not only to the members of those Christian communities, but also to millions of viewers on Sunday mornings.

Our God is not a Silent God!

Many people are trying to find their way in the dark. Many of them pray, but they complain of the silence of God. They cannot hear him speaking to them. Well, a long time ago, Paul wrote to the Hebrews: 'At various times in the past and in various different ways, God spoke to our ancestors through the prophets, but in our own time, the last days, he has spoken to us through his Son...'(Heb 1:1-2).

And at the beginning of the Gospel of John we read: 'The Word was made flesh, he lived among us'. God has said everything in his Son! The first Christian communities, led by the apostles and by the Holy Spirit, reinterpreted the life and message of Jesus Christ in the light of the resurrection and the evangelists wrote the essential core of those meditations down for us — the Gospels.

A Love Letter sent by the Holy Spirit

We have a priceless treasure in the Bible. And a special treasure is the Gospel — that love letter sent by the Holy Spirit to the churches, to the Church and to each one of us.

If you receive a love letter, do you keep it unopened? Surely not! You open it at once and read it and then you read it again and again! And what a deep experience it is! You read it, after all, not just with your eyes of flesh, but also with the eyes of your heart. In this way you come, through the medium of words, into the presence of the person you love and are united with him or her.

Going to the Gospel is going into the presence of someone who has come into our presence. It is coming close to him, discovering him with the 'eyes' of faith, knowing him and recognising him, being united with him and having communion with him.

If we love, we want to make ourselves known to the one we love. By means of the Gospel, Jesus wants to make himself known and also to make his Father and his Father's infinite love known. Doing without that encounter is failing to be really Christian.

How Should we Read and Mediate on the Gospel?

It is quite right, of course, that we should try to situate the Gospels within their historical context, study their composition and so on. But we should not let that task take the place of our faith and our love. Nor should the way of faith and love become a way of self-interest. We should not go to the Gospel seeking clear and immediate solutions to all the problems in our lives. We have to go, as it were, gratuitously. If we come into Jesus' presence through Scripture and see him there living, acting, reacting and speaking, we shall gradually learn to think as he does and to behave with the actions of the Gospel. For the Word is seed and it is in our lives that it will grow and bear fruit.

Reading the Gospel in Church

These love letters were first sent by the Holy Spirit to the Church and the Church has kept them as though they were a treasure beyond price. It is the Church that offers them to us now. Happy are those who can meditate on Scripture with others, in little groups in local church communities within the great universal Church and then share the fruits of their prayer with others!

The Word of God is living, Paul tells us. So, in our own way, we too receive the good news of Jesus and offer to others the good news of our own lives, inflamed with love.

Michel Quoist
June 1985

1

*Meeting God, fine, but how and where?**

Everyone who believes, whatever his religion is, tries to come close to God and meet him. Obviously, you are all people like that. Yet can any one of you honestly say: 'I have met God'? Of course not.

Don't be afraid to admit it. Long before you were here, Jesus himself declared: 'No one has seen the Father'. But when one of his apostles, Philip, asked him, he said: 'To have seen me is to have seen the Father' and added: 'You must believe me when I say that I am in the Father and the Father is in me' (John 14:9, 10). The apostles believed this — not of their own accord, but enlightened by the Holy spirit.

Our Muslim friends go part of the way with us. They see Jesus as a great prophet. We go further and believe God came to meet us in Jesus of Nazareth. We believe he is the 'image of the unseen God', as Paul wrote to the Colossians, We belive he is 'the Way, the

*Homily for the 6th Sunday of Eastertide, Cycle A.

1

Truth and the Life' and that 'no one can come to the Father except through him'.

If we want to meet God, we must meet Jesus Christ. But how and where? That is what I want to tell you.

Jesus Christ is present, but how?

First of all, how is Jesus Christ present among us today?

There are many different ways of being present with each other and our physical presence is not necessarily the only way of judging whether we are really united as persons. We can be side by side and even touching one another and yet be quite separate. Couples whose mariage is under stress know that only too well! What unites us is love, because love is a gift from one to another, it is communion with one another.

Let me give you an example. I would like to speak especially to the mothers, because it is their feast today. Have you never said or thought of saying to one of your children who is going a long way from home at a critical time in his or her life: 'Good-bye, my dearest one, I am going with you! I will be with you every day, whatever happens to you.' And, of course, you are present! Not physically, but with that mysterious presence of love that can cross space and

2

even time. Not even death can separate those who really love one another, because love cannot die.

The risen Jesus is present with us, with a mysterious presence of love that goes beyond all human love, because his Love is infinite. Like a mother who is overflowing with tenderness for her children, he goes with us. And he will always be with us in his Spirit of Love. he has told us, after all: 'I will not leave you orphans.'

Jesus Christ is present, but where?

Where can we be sure of meeting the living Jesus? There is a simple answer to that question: where he said he would be. Let me give you four statements that he made indicating this.

The first points to the community of all who believe. Jesus said: 'Where two or three meet in my name, I shall be there with them' (Matt. 18:20). Those two or three are you — husbands and wives united in love. Your love is offered freely to the Lord so that he can fill it with a new dimension, that of eternity. Christ is there when you love one another in his sight and it would not be wrong to say the more you love each other, the more he is present. And that community of 'two or three' is also any little group of Christians meeting together to pray or think about

3

their faith and their lives, a little class of children gathered together to learn about their faith or the parish... Two or three... a little community. The Church... that great community. He is there. He has told us.

The second of Jesus' statements is about the heart of one who loves his brothers. Saint John tells us, when the Lord was saying farewell to his apostles, he told them: 'I give you a new commandment: love one another; just as I have loved you, you must also love one another' and a little later he added: 'If anyone loves me he will keep my word and my Father will love him and we shall come to him and make our home with him' (John 13:34; 14:23).

A young man I used to know was filled with happiness when he first heard this promise and began to look for God. But he believed that God was a long way away. Then slowly he discovered that, if he loved his brothers, God would come to him and, if he tried to be really open to God's Love, he could — supreme witness, this — lend Jesus his hand to clasp his brothers' hands, his face to smile at and his head and arms to serve them 'If anyone loves me he will keep my word and my Father will love him and we shall come to him and make our home with him.'

The third statement consists of the words, signs and actions that the Lord left us when he entrusted them to his Church. I mean, of course, the sacraments and above all that sign at the centre of our Christian lives, the Eucharist.

I would like to give you two images. We have invented many gestures so that we can give each other not only the best of ourselves, but also, unfortunately, the worst. We have inbented handshaking, for example, as an offer of friendship. But is it always a gesture of friendship? We have also invented another magnificent sign: the kiss. You know, of course, what it means when two people who really love each other are parting for a long time! Their kiss means: we cannot make up our minds to separate without giving ourselves to each other, so we have to try to have communion with each other. So, my love, I am taking you with me and you are taking me with you! But I would ask you, my friends: do you always share the whole of your life in your kisses?

Jesus also invented actions so that he could give his Love to those who wanted to receive it. But in his case we can be sure he gives everything he has promised to give in those gestures.

It was the last evening that he was sharing a meal with his apostles and he was getting ready to leave them. Their parting was as painful as the circumstances were tragic. He was going to be arrested, tortured and put to death. He knew that. He could

5

not make up his mind to go away. So he invented a way of staying with them — with us. He took bread and wine and shared it with them. 'This is my Body', he said; 'this is my Blood, shed for you', adding: 'Do this is memory of me.'

This means, for us Christians: every time you share the bread and wine in community, in the Church, with a priest representing me — that is, making me present again, you can be certain I shall be there through that gesture, that sign. I shall be there with my body, with my heart, with the gift of my life. And, if you want to, you can have communion with that life.

Finally, the fourth statement I promised to give you. This one is about the poor and the 'least of the brothers'.

Jesus forewarned us when he said: 'I was hungry, I was thirsty, I was a stranger, naked, sick, in prison, and you cared for me . . . or you did not care for me' and we protest: 'Lord, when did we see you hungry, thirsty, a stranger, naked, sick or in prison?' And he will answer: 'The poor and the least of these brothers of mine . . . Do you remember? They were me!' (see Matt. 25:31-46).

Do I need to say that 'I was hungry' means not only 'I was hungry for bread', but also perhaps 'I was hungry for friendship, for love, hungry to continue my studies, hungry for responsibility'. That 'I was in prison' means just that, 'I was in prison', but it may also mean: 'I was afraid to express myself' or 'I was enslaved to work that I had not chosen to do' . . . And the Lord will say to us: 'What did you do for me?'

So in the Gospel Jesus identified himself first with bread and wine and secondly with the poor and the 'least of the brothers'. I know — and I have to say this to reassure the theologians — it is not exactly the same 'presence' that is expressed in these two cases, but I know too that both express a very real presence, in so far as we cannot have communion in the Eucharist if we do not have communion with our brothers.

So there you are! We are all looking for God, but do we not often look where he is not, when in fact he is on the road we follow every day? And if we do not 'see' him, it is perhaps because we are, like the people in the Gospel, blind and we have to be healed of our blindness?

O Jesus Christ, open our eyes, you who are the 'image of the unseen God', and we shall 'see' you and meet you living — in the community of those who believe, in the faithfulness of our loving hearts and in the signs, the sacraments you have left us. And we shall come to know you have no other face for us than the face of our brothers.

2

Is being a Christian dangerous?[*]

The Gospel of Jesus Christ according to Saint Matthew — 10:26-33

Jesus instructed the Apostles, saying

Do not be afraid. For everything that is now covered will be uncovered and everything now hidden will be made clear. What I say to you in the dark, tell in the daylight; what you hear in whispers, proclaim from the housetops.

Do not be afraid of those who kill the body, but cannot kill the soul; fear him rather who can destroy both body and soul in hell. Can you not buy two sparrows for a penny? And yet not one falls to the ground without your Father knowing. Why, every hair on your head has been counted. So there is no need to be afraid; you are worth more than hundreds of sparrows.

[*]Homily for the 12th Sunday in Ordinary Time, Cycle A.

So if anyone declares himself for me in the presence of men, I will declare myself for him in the presence of my Father in heaven. But the one who disowns me in the presence of men, I will disown in the the presence of my Father in heaven.

Being a disciple of Jesus Christ is not easy! In this passage of the Gospel — and in those that precede and follow it — the Lord warns us very clearly that we are likely to be persecuted if we follow him.

You may think, of course, that this is an exaggeration. It may apply to Christians living in the Eastern block or in Latin America, but not to us! We are not marked out and our names are not noted down because we have come to church this morning or because we have followed a service on radio or television. We don't have to feel anxious, either, like those in some countries during the war, who closed the doors, listened to the news on the English radio and risked being denounced to the occupying forces.

Living the Gospel is not a sinecure!
Going to Mass on Sunday morning, not deceiving my husband or my wife, not taking my neighbour's bank card, putting a little silver in the envelope for the fight against world poverty and thinking about the

mystery of the Trinity in the depths of my heart! If that is all being a disciple of Jesus Christ means, there is every chance I would not feel anxious! But if being a disciple of Jesus Christ is not just 'practising a religion', but also 'practising the Gospel' — in other words, living the Gospel in the whole of my life? In that case, I am likely to be very anxious and many things in my life will be put into perspective. Why is that?

It is because living the Gospel is first and foremost bearing witness by what one says and does that Jesus is alive and that he can transform our lives and the life of the world. And it is also working with him to bring about this transformation. It is loving others as we love ourselves, in other words, wanting for them what we want for ourselves and therefore knowing that we cannot be happy in isolation. It is wanting to build up a world in which all our brothers can grow as men and as sons of God.

Let us be realistic. Whoever sets off on that road will have to struggle. But it will not just be any struggle, since fighting together with Jesus is fighting people while respecting and even loving them. It is also accepting that we will be attacked on two other fronts — on the one hand by those who claim that it is not Christian to fight and, on the other, by those who insist that we have to fight and use any means available to us to settle human problems.

The disciples of Jesus Christ are afraid

We are afraid, let us admit it, of taking part in this struggle. That is understandable! We are afraid of the risk to our family, our situation in life, our peace of mind, afraid we shall be misinterpreted, rejected, persecuted...

Only this week a young executive was telling me about a very unjust situation in his company and said: 'I dare not speak out in case I lose my job or my chance of promotion!' A student nurse told me recently: 'The other day I witnessed very unprofessional behavious on the part of a qualified nurse, but how could I say anything? I might have been given a bad report and the exam is in a few weeks' time.' A trade union activist was complaining to me; 'I do not agree at all with the methods my union is using in our present campaign, but I don't want to set the lads against me, so I am saying nothing.'

We are afraid. Well, the Lord tells us again and again: 'Do not be afraid!' and he uses two arguments to put our minds at rest. The first is: What makes you afraid is not essential. The second is: You have nothing to fear, because I am there and I love you.

We are mistaken about fear

In the first place, then, what makes us afraid is not essential. I am afraid for my body, in other words, for everything material in my life. But Jesus said: Do not be afraid of what may harm your body, so long as your soul is not affected. Only fear what may harm the soul as well as the body! — That means: everything in you that makes you human. What is really bad is to be so harmed or destroyed that you are no longer the image of God — that image that you are now and should become more and more each day. It would be tragic if you were no longer that son on whom the Father relies absolutely to bear witness to his love and to continue the mission of his Son Jesus on earth.

In fact, the Lord is once again asking us: What are the essential values for you? What are you really fighting for? What are you really afraid of losing? What you really value is revealed by the nature of your fears.

Ought we not to examine our consciences in order to re-orientate our lives, our efforts and our struggles towards what is essential: living the Gospel in all its dimensions? If we do that, we shall, of course, have to suffer. We may perhaps not succeed so well materially. We may often be misunderstood. But —

and this is my last point — the Lord has said: Do not be afraid, because I am there.

Nothing escapes the Father's attention

He said this in two images. They are both quite unexpected, but we must try to understand them.

First the sparrows. They cost very little — ten a penny! But 'not one falls to the gound without your Father knowing.' Then 'Every hair on your head has been counted. So there is no need to be afraid.' Then: 'You are worth more than hundreds of sparrows.'

What should I say about this? That God directs everything from heaven? That he condemns a little bird to death and then another when he wants to and that we lose our hair because he wants us to and he is more powerful than any magic hair lotion and likes to be methodical in his work of making us bald? There is only one conclusion to draw from that interpretation: Let events take their course and let us submit to the will of God.

But that is not the right interpretation! God is not a dictator with absolute power whose slaves, men and women, can do or say nothing when he directs them from far off. Jesus Christ has revealed to us that God is a Father and he tells us in today's Gospel that he is such a loving and watchful Father that nothing that happens to each one of us ever escapes his attention. He cares in this way for all his creation, but even more for his beloved children. We are worth so much to him that he sent his own Son to redeem us!

The true disciple of Jesus Christ cannot be harmed

But that does not mean we are not hurt in the struggle. God has not given us a miraculous bullet-proof vest to wear, nor does he ever send his toughest angels to act as our body-guards. We shall be harmed like everyone else, but the wounds will not penetrate to our heart of hearts. We shall remain peaceful and loving because we are made strong by a Love that transcends us, a Love that has triumphed over hatred, suffering and death. We cannot be harmed.

So do not be afraid! Do not be ashamed of Jesus Christ. Let us join in the fray with him. Let us leave the spectators in the seats and enter the arena with those engaged in the struggle. God has given us a world to build and all our brothers to love. With Jesus, we shall build the Kingdom!

Do not be afraid! The Father is very close to each one of us and his eyes never leave us. He even cares about the hair that has fallen on your shoulder.

3

'Love one another
as I have loved you'*

The Gospel of Jesus Christ according to John — 15:9-17

[On the eve of his crucifixion, Jesus instructed his disciples:]

As the Father has loved me, so I have loved you. Remain in my love. If you keep my commandments you will remain in my love, just as I have kept my Father's commandments and remain in his love. I have told you this so that my own joy may be in you and your joy be complete. This is my commandment: love one another, as I have loved you.

A man can have no greater love than to lay down his life for his friends. You are my friends, if you do what I command you. I shall not call you servants any more, because a servant does not know his

*Homily for the 6th Sunday of Eastertide, Cycle B.

master's business; I call you friends, because I have made known to you everything I have learnt from my Father.

You did not choose me, no, I chose you; and I commissioned you to go out and bear fruit, fruit that will last; and then the Father will give you anything you ask him in my name.

What I command you is to love one another.

Why are we alive? Why do we train for a profession? Why do we get up each morning and go to work? Why do we get married, create a home, have children? And then, later in life, sit in an armchair waiting for death? Why, my friends? What is our life? What is man? Where do we come from? Where are we going? Are we just hanging in space? Do we come from nowhere and are we going nowhere? Are we just little sparks of life that came about by chance, sufficiently conscious to know that we are alive and that our life is absurd? What a terrible fate! A flower is beautiful. It does not know why, but at least it cannot ask why! It does not know that it exists. But we do.

Who makes man live?
May I confide in you? When I was a young man, I

tried to find an answer to these fundamental questions. I looked at 'man' and tried to discover the deepest and most universal force present in him. 'As soon as I have found that,' I thought, 'I shall go upstream and find the source of life.' My first reaction was that it all depended on a will to live and a fundamental need to defend life and help it to develop. But gradually I discovered another force in man's heart that was much stronger than the will to live — love. So strong was the power of that love, I found, that man was able to sacrifice his life. From then on, I did not just look at man living — I also looked at him loving and I saw that all love gave life. I had found the source! Faith had revealed it to me in all its infinite dimensions.

We are made by love to love

In today's Gospel, Jesus Christ makes the most astonishing declaration of love: 'I love you as the Father loves me.' That means: 'I love you infinitely.' However young or old we are, whatever our race, our culture, our environment may be and however we may have behaved yesterday or will behave today or tomorrow — God loves us and has always loved us. Saint Paul says that, even before the world was made,

God thought of us in his Love. We are his thoughts of love made flesh! That force of love dormant in each one of us is the Father breathing his love on us and giving us life by loving us every moment of our existence. Believing in that Love is the first step that we have to take in faith. It sets us free from the absurdity of living without being born to love and without a father! It breaks through our solitude and frees us from existential anxiety, from the thought that we exist without reason. We are made by love to love.

'Remain in my love'

But it is not enough for us simply to be conscious of the love that has created us. We have to respond to it. I spoke about a flower just now. It is a flower without being conscious of its existence. It lives without knowing why, without wanting to and without a reason for living. We can consciously and freely let ourselves be loved and let ourselves be fully created. Man is the only one of God's creatures who can take part in his own creation.

How can a river continue to flow if it is cut off from its source? How can man continue to live if he rejects God? Yet he is so foolish today that he looks for the reason for living in himself alone. But surely he is condemning himself to slow death!

And what about us? We think we can look at God and call him Father. We think that we are really alive because he loves us. But are we always ready to set aside a few moments, not to assault God with our many requests, but to stay in his presence, silent, recollected, without moving, letting ourselves be loved and created?

Jesus tells us today: 'Remain in my love.' But take care! There is one essential condition for remaining in that love and that is we must be faithful to the Lord's commandment: 'Love one another as I have loved you'. We can only remain in God's love if we love our brothers as God loves them. And when God loves, he both expresses and proves it.

Jesus Christ reveals God's love

In the first place, he expresses it. He has not remained silent! He came to reveal his very nature to us in Jesus Christ: 'God is love'. He came to tell us that he is our Father and that he loves us. Do we 'reveal' our love to those we love?

Let me tell you a story. A man came to see me recently. 'I am just recovering from a terrible car accident,' he said. 'The panels of our crushed car had closed up and I and my son were trapped. I called to him, but he did not answer. I managed to get hold of his hand. His pulse was just beating, but he did not answer me when I spoke. Then, in my distress, I suddenly thought: "I have never once told him I love him." This thought began to obsess me. "Supposing he dies before I can tell him! Let him regain consciousness for a moment at least! Let him not die until he knows I love him!"

'Much later, in the hospital, I heard him sigh and then murmur a few words. So I dragged myself to his bed and on my knees beside him I whispered: "It's your dad, son. I love you so much..."' And my friend ended his story: 'My son is alive and he knows his father loves him because I told him.'

'Reveal' your love to those you love

Do you 'reveal' your love to those you love? Perhaps you say they know already! But surely they need to hear you say it? It is tragic that there are so many people on earth who have no one to whisper to them: 'I love you.' How are we to live if we do not live *for* anyone? How are we to live if no one tells us: 'I need you'? Loving is, after all, giving our life to another and receiving it from that other.

God loves and proves it

God is not satisfied with just expressing his love. In the second place, he also proves it. He proves it in the most radical way — in solidarity with us to the point of death. In his own words: 'A man can have no greater love than to lay down his life for his friends.' Giving one's life to others — to all others — is, in a sense, telling them: 'Your lives are so valuable to me that I am sacrificing mine for yours.' That action is the only irrefutable proof of the authenticity of one's declarations of love and indeed of all one's good, generous intentions.

How are we to give our lives to those we love?

We should not think that 'giving one's life' is an action to be confined to a few heroes whose names are engraved in gold letters on public monuments!

If you are a mother, giving your life may be getting up several times in the night when your baby is crying. If you are a father, it may be getting up every morning and going off to work to earn money for your family. Giving your life may also be taking an active part in a parent-teacher association, a trade union, a political party or a group for social action, so that your brothers and sisters may have a more human life. Giving your life may sometimes be fighting or engaging in conflict, but it may also be just giving someone a smile, clasping their hand or giving them ten minutes of your time — ten minutes of your life without being paid for it, for someone who is lonely.

But I have been told: 'Many people give their lives like that, but would not call themselves Christians.' What is it, then, that distinguishes the Christian?

The Christian, my friends — and this is where I conclude my sermon — is the man or woman who has heard God say: 'I love you.' It is the person who believes with all his heart in that infinite love of God, is completely open to receive it and, turning towards his brothers and sisters, hands that Love on to them, giving them his life.

4

Jesus Christ offers himself as food *

The Gospel of Jesus Christ according to Saint John — 6:41-51

Meanwhile the Jews were complaining to each other about him, because he had said, "I am the bread that came down from heaven." "Surely this is Jesus the son of Joseph," they said. "We know his father and mother. How can he now say, 'I have come down from heaven'?" Jesus said in reply, "Stop complaining to each other. No one can come to me unless he is drawn by the Father who sent me, and I will raise him up on the last day.

"It is written in the prophets: They will all be taught by God, and to hear the teaching of the Father and learn from it is to come to me. Not that anybody has seen the father, except the one who comes from God: he has seen the Father.

"I tell you most solemnly, everyone who believes

*Homily for the 19th Sunday in Ordinary Time, Cycle B.

23

has eternal life. I am the bread of life. Your fathers ate manna in the desert and they are dead; but this is the bread that comes down from heaven, so that a man may eat it and not die. I am the living bread that has come down from heaven. Anyone who eats this bread will live for ever; and the bread that I shall give is my flesh, for the life of the world."

This Gospel forms part of a long discourse on the bread of life. It looks forward to the Eucharist and is the continuation of the story of the miracles of the loaves.

Ordinary bread or bread of life?

The evangelist tells us that the people came back again on the day after that miracle, looking for Jesus. That is hardly surprising! On the day before, they had all eaten their fill! No need to pay, go shopping or cook! That is what you all dream about, isn't it, you wives and mothers? And the whole atmosphere was so good — it was nice to listen to someone speaking so well during a meal!

But on the next day, it was not so good! The same crowd of people, probably great numbers of them, were disappointed to find no free open air meal — nothing at all to eat, not even shellfish from the Sea of

Galilee, only words. And what words! Only Jesus expressing those very disconcerting ideas that made freethinkers call him mad, but filled the poor and lowly, those whose hearts were pure, with joy. 'Make no mistake about it!' Jesus declared on that day. 'I have not come to fill you with bread, but to offer myself as food. I am the living bread which has come down from heaven. Anyone who eats this bread will live for ever.'

You know how the story goes on. The crowd reacted in various ways, with laughter, anger or commiseration. 'Surely this is Jesus, son of Joseph. We know his father and mother. How can he now say, "I have come down from heaven"?' And the evangelist concludes: 'After this, many of his disciples left him and stopped going with him.'

What do we want from Jesus Christ?

What would we have done in that situation? And what do we expect from Jesus? Do we perhaps too often regard him as a super-director of an employment agency, a person with mysterious powers at the top of a wealthy charitable organisation or a doctor with miraculous cures? What do we want from him? A job? A good salary? Success in an exam? A cure for our aches and pains? It is not wrong to ask him for those things, but if we confine ourselves to them, we shall be like the young woman who looks first at her lover's hands every time she sees him and asks, aloud or silently: 'What have you got for me today?' Instead of looking into his eyes and saying, aloud or silently: Thank you for being there for me. Thank you for giving your life to me.' For loving is not giving 'things'. It is above all giving oneself as food to those one loves.

Many of us might think as those who heard Jesus two thousand years ago must have thought: 'It is too difficult to understand straightaway, but if we reflect about it, we may grasp what he is saying.' When they gave us life, our parents gave us their hearts, but in a sense they also gave us their bodies. Two brothers told me the other day: 'Our mother gave us everything. She gave us her health.' These two men knew they had, in a sense, been fed by their mother's life. And today, as yesterday, Christ offers us his life, so that the world may live, so that we may live and so that we may live eternally.

Present with everyone and everything
But how it is possible for Jesus Christ to give his life to all his brothers? How can he be present with each one of us and in the whole of human history,

yesterday, today and tomorrow? To help you to understand, I would say first of all that there are different ways of being present with one another and secondly that Christ invented a number of signs or actions, which he used in order to give himself completely to those who wanted to receive him.

First, then, there are different ways of being present with those we love. We can be physically present with the one we love, or, on the other hand, we can find each other in a mysterious way even if we are separated by a great distance. Every love must surely have said or written at some time: 'I was with you the other day, my darling, during that ordeal . . that happy experience.' And it is true, they were together. He was there and she was there. The bonds that unite those who love one another go beyond bodies touching or embracing and neither time nor space nor even death can loosen them.

The actions in which Jesus gives himself

Secondly, Christ has invented certain actions or signs into which he has entered completely so that he can continue to offer himself to the Father, the world and us. These are the sacraments and especially the Eucharist.

We have also invented signs and gestures in order to

show others the best of ourselves. We have invented the handclasp as a gesture of our gift of friendship and the kiss so that we can give each other our love. You must, like me, have seen couples on railway platforms, one seeing the other off on a main line train, devouring each other with their eyes. As soon as they hear the signal, they come together in an embrace that lasts until almost too late. What a beautiful gesture that is! And you know, of course, what it means: I cannot bring myself to part from you. I want to say with you and I want you to stay with me. So I am trying to have communion with you, just as you are trying to have communion with me.' But at the same time, you know as well as I do that we do not put ourselves completely into the gestures we have invented. Do we always give our friendship when we give another our hand? And do lovers always give all their love in every kiss? The signs unfortunately often have no content and are no more than counter-signs.

But Christ offers himself completely in the actions that he wanted to institute so that he could remain with us. What he said to us was: 'When you come together as a community, as a Church, one of you, chosen and consecrated to pronounce my words and perform my actions again, will share the bread and wine with the others and I promise you that I shall be there, present in a real presence, with my body, my heart and the whole of my being, and I shall give myself to you as food in order to give you life.

What are we looking for?

What are we looking for? Our daily bread? We are right to look for that. Jesus himself told us to ask for it every day. But do we not perhaps cover it too thickly with rich butter that gradually undermines our health, introduces chloresterol into our blood and even threatens our heart? What, then, really concerns us most? Where do we look for happiness?

I have met many young people who reject the material benefits that so often almost prevent us from living. They are not mad or idle. On the contrary, they may have exaggerated or vague ideas, but do they not confront us with essential questions: What is the meaning of our life? What are our values? What kind of world are we bulding?

Should we not be looking, in and beyond our fears and anxieties for the future, our revolts and our deepest aspirations, for what Christ has offered us for almost two thousand years: his life so that we and the world may live?

5

*The feast of the living**

The Gospel of Jesus Christ according to Saint Matthew — 5:1-12

Seeing the crowds, Jesus went up the hill. There he sat down and was joined by his disciples. Then he began to speak. This is what he taught them:

"How happy are the poor in spirit;
theirs is the kingdom of heaven.
Happy *the gentle:*
they shall have the earth for their heritage.
Happy those who mourn:
they shall be comforted.
Happy those who hunger and thirst for what is right:
they shall be satisfied.
Happy are the merciful:
they shall have mercy shown to them.
Happy the pure in heart:

*Homily for the Feast of All Saints.

they shall see God.
Happy the peacemakers:
they shall be called sons of God.
Happy those who are persecuted in the cause
of right:
theirs is the kingdom of heaven.
Happy are you when people abuse you and
persecute you and speak all kinds of calumny
against you on my account. Rejoice and be glad, for
your reward will be in heaven; this is how they
persecuted the prophets before you.''

Try to imagine a very united family with so many
children that it had become impossible to celebrate
each one's birthday separately and so it had been
decided to hold one birthday feast for all of them
together. That family is the Church and the feast is
All Saints. All Saints is, after all, the feast of the living.
It is the feast of all who are living in Christ the
eternity of Love.

Tomorrow, on 2 November, we are invited to pray
for all those who have died, so that they may also join
that 'huge number, impossible to count, of people
from every nation, race, tribe and language' of whom
Saint John spoke in the first reading today (Rev. 7:9).
So now I shall combine in this sermon the liturgy of

31

today, All Saints, with the liturgy of tomorrow, All Souls.

Is death — the death of those we love and our own death — a tragic and shocking end point? Or is it, as Teresa of Lisieux put it so magnificently, an 'entry into life'?

Some people, I know, are still looking for an answer. They have doubts and they suffer. I do not want to dry anyone's tears this morning, because Jesus himself wept at his friend's death, but I would like those who are weeping not to weep in the same way as those who are, in the words of Saint Paul, 'without hope'.

Our dead are living

Scripture tells us our dead are living. But some will say: You tell me and my faith tells me they are living, but I have seen my dear ones die and I do not see them alive any more. So I suffer. And you are right, of course. We all want to see, touch and hold those we love and only a body can be embraced. But did you only love a body? Our eyes and our lips can deceive us, but our heart cannot! And only our heart is able to reach the 'life after death' of those we love.

I was called recently to the bedside of a dying man. He was very old and his face was ravaged and distorted by illness and suffering. I watched his wife. She was leaning over him, caressing him and whispering to him... such tender words: 'How beautiful you are, my love, how fine you look!' I was very embarrassed and thought: 'How can anyone be so blind?... Love is blind!'

Then an extraordinary thing happened. As she caressed him, the old man half-opened his eyes and a hesitant smile appeared on his face. He looked at his wife for a long time and she looked at him. There was a mysterious communion between them. And his smile spread. It was like the sun after a storm. I saw it. I know that I saw what she saw! She was right — the old man, made ugly by suffering, was beautiful. Love is not blind. No, love lets us see what others do not see.

That woman was guided by love to go beyond the deep wrinkles of her husband's suffering old face and had joined someone who was beyond, far beyond the body, someone who could not die even if his body were to crumble away in her sight and finally disappear.

What is death and what is life?

But if what is essential in man cannot die, what is death? Death, real death, is already in our life. Death is when we cease not to live but to love. 'Whoever keeps my word,' Jesus said, 'will never see death' (John 8:51) and Paul insisted that it was man who brought death into the world through sin (Rom. 5:12). If we love, as Jesus has asked us to, we shall live eternally.

Eternal life does not, moreover, begin after our life here on earth. It is not the last stage of a rocket projected into space and destined to orbit eternally. Eternal life is already with us. Saint Paul says that whoever is united to Christ has already been brought to life and raised up with him and has been given a place with him in heaven (see Eph. 2:6 and Col. 2:12).

Eternal life is not a different life replacing our present life. It is our everyday life lived in Christ and it will open out finally and definitively when love has completedly penetrated the whole of our being and can finally produce the fruit of which it has only been the seed.

The promises of love, then, will be kept. In the risen Christ all loneliness will finally be broken through. The long search for others will be definitively ended in complete union. We shall live beyond the body. Our bodies will no longer be an obstacle and we shall be handed over entirely to the joy of loving. Heaven is loving everyone and everything in Christ in the rhythm of the Trinity.

We would like to see and to be able to imagine

We believe as Christians in that life of Christ at the heart of our life, but we would like to see. It is, however, just not possible! As Paul says: 'The life you have is hidden with Christ in God, but when Christ is revealed — and he is your life — you too will be revealed in all your glory with him' (Col. 3:1-4).

We believe that our dead are living and that we shall also live, but we would like to be able to imagine how. But again, it is not possible! The Christian is like a little child in his mother's lap. He is alive, he may be warm or cold and he knows that, but he cannot imagine that he will one day see the sky, the mountains and the forests or that he will discover the joy of being loved in his mothers's eyes. He has to go through death to reach that life. Paul replied to the Christians of Corinth, when they asked him about the bodies they whould have in eternity: 'They are stupid questions!' and then asked them in turn whether they had any ideas of the harvest when they sowed seed, which had to die before it was given new life. A 'biological body', he insisted, was sown and a 'spiritual body' was raised (1 Cor. 15:35ff.) and by that he meant a body entirely at the service of the spirit, a transfigured body. Our bodies, which are now opaque and hard, will become translucent and shining when they are penetrated by the light.

Where shall we meet our dead?

Many people go to the cemetery on this feast to visit the graves of their loved ones after celebrating the Eucharist. Some find it a deeply peaceful experience of faith, but for others it is painful and unhappy, a journey through the night of doubt. But for everyone it is an opportunity to come close to those whom they can no longer reach with their eyes and their lips.

But is it really at the cemetery that we meet our dead? No, surely not. Their bodies have returned to the earth from which they came, just a little of ourselves returns each day to the earth that feeds us.

No, we meet our dead when we meet Christ. Our dead are living! But they are living in him, who has conquered death. In him we are close to them and in him they can benefit from our love and we can benefit from theirs. Oh, the physical absence of those we love is painful, of course, and for some of us almost impossible to bear, but I would like to tell you with all the strength of my Christian faith that it is not an obstacle to meeting them and being united with them.

Let me finish with a second story. Shortly after the end of the war, a married couple came to me for counsel. Their love had withered away and the marriage had become a tragedy. Hard words were exchanged between them in my presence and they criticised each other mercilessly. Suddenly the wife seized hold of her husband's arm and pulled quite violently at it. Her eyes were full of tears and she cried: 'We were closer to each other in the war, when you were a prisoner in Poland!' And it was true — since the war, they had been close enough to touch, but they were in fact very far away from one another. So what separates us is surely a lack of love, not physical distance or death.

I would like to conclude with these words: If you are more closely united with Christ today than you were yesterday and if you have a deeper experience of his Love, then you must be closer to your dear ones who are dead than you were when you were able to touch and hold them. That is because all of us who are on our way in this world and all those who have gone ahead of us on the same way are members of the same body, in which the same life circulates like blood. And that life is the life of the risen Christ and only Love can measure the depth of our union with him and our fellow-men. So, do not weep today like those who are without hope!

6

*Jesus, the Pharisee and the sinful woman (the prostitute)**

The Gospel of Jesus Christ according to Saint Luke —
7:36-50

One of the Pharisees invited him to a meal. When
he arrived at the Pharisee's house and took his place
at table, a woman came in, who had a bad name in
the town. She had heard he was dining with the
Pharisee and had brought with her an alabaster jar
of ointment. She waited behind him at his feet,
weeping, and her tears fell on his feet and she wiped
them away with her hair; then she covered his feet
with kisses and anointed them with the ointment.

When the Pharisee who had invited him saw this,
he said to himself, "If this man were a prophet, he
would know who this woman is who is touching
him and what a bad name she has". Then Jesus
took him up and said, "Simon, I have something to
say to you". "Speak Master" was the reply. "There

*Homily for the 11th Sunday in Ordinary Time, Cycle C.

was once a creditor who had two men in his debt; one owed him five hundred denarii, the other fifty. They were unable to pay, so he pardoned them both. Which of them will love him more?" "The one who was pardoned more, I suppose" answered Simon. Jesus said, "You are right".

Then he turned to the woman. "Simon," he said "you see this woman? I came into your house and you poured no water over my feet, but she has poured out her tears over my feet and wiped them away with her hair. You gave me no kiss, but she has been covering my feet with kisses ever since I came in. You did not anoint my head with oil, but she has anointed my feet with ointment. For this reason I tell you that her sins, her many sins, must have been forgiven her or she would not have shown such great love. It is the man who is forgiven little who shows little love." Then he said to her, "Your sins are forgiven." Those who were with him at table began to say to themselves, "Who is this man, that he even forgives sins?" But he said to the woman, "Your faith has saved you; go in peace".

It is scandalous! Here we have a pious man who practised his religion and was zealous in his observance of the Law inviting Jesus to a meal and then being sharply rebuked by him. And at the same time Jesus commends a prostitute, whose scandalous way of life was known to everyone and who had no respect for religion or morality. Not only does he hold her up as an example — he also forgives her in a single sentence her sinful, disordered way of life! How discouraging for good, orthodox people! What do you have to say?

I think I know what you will say. That is because you know the Gospel story. You will be on the Lord's side. 'He came to save sinners,' you will say. 'He said himself that it is the sick, not those who are well who need the doctor.' In order words, you expect and admire Jesus for his attitude — yesterday. But do you accept the attitude of the Church today? Be honest — do you not say or at least think sometimes: 'More fuss is made in the Church now of sinners and marginalised people than of us practising believers,' or 'Some priests forgive everything and everybody in the name of love,' or 'No one respects the Church's moral and religious teachings nowadays.'

Are we not all a bit pharisaical? We think quite highly of ourselves among our fellow-men, but we can hardly bear to have those whom we regard as having gone astray and sinned forgiven. So let us try to understand what Jesus is telling us in this Gospel.

To help you to understand, I will say three things about this story: firstly, Jesus looks into our hearts and not at our actions; secondly, forgiving is loving perfectly and thirdly, only faith can save us.

Jesus looks into our hearts, not at our actions

Jesus did not condemn the Pharisees because they were faithful to the Law and their religious practices. He condemned them for clinging so scrupulously to those laws and practices when they had become devoid of life and love. Jesus looks into our hearts, not at our actions. That does not mean he is against actions. After all, he rebukes Simon, the 'righteous' man, because he had provided no little touches of hospitality of the kind that reveal an authentic love, whereas the sinful woman had, despite her poverty, lavished them on him. What did he say to Simon? 'I came into your house and you poured no water over my feet, but she has poured out her tears over my feet and wiped them away with her hair. You gave me no kiss, but she has been covering my feet with kisses ever since I came in. You did not anoint my head with oil . . . '

But we should not think that Simon was indifferent to Jesus. He was obviously drawn to him, because he invited him to his home. But he could not understand the sinful woman, nor could he understand Jesus' attitude towards her. This is because, although he had opened the door of his house, he had not opened his heart. In fact, he did not believe in man. Nor did he believe in Jesus Christ's love for man. He did not believe that love could transform everything. He did not believe that for Jesus no one was lost for ever. Simon the Pharisee enclosed the sinful woman in her past. Jesus opened her to her future.

How do we react to this? Let us be honest, bearing in mind how often we are disconcerted or scandalised by the moral or religious behaviour of so many of our brothers and sisters in Christ, especially the younger ones. Do we not all too often regard those whose behaviour we do not understand as unforgivable sinners? But before we judge them, should we not try to find out why they are behaving like that? And, even if we cannot objectively accept certain attitudes or situations, ought we not to accept unconditionally the people themselves? If they are to live or come to life again, they need to be understood and forgiven. To condemn them for ever is always wrong!

But take note, my friends. In the Gospel story, it is the 'righteous' man who judges and condemns and who is in turn judged and condemned, and the sinful woman who is saved.

Forgiving is loving perfectly

Forgiveness is the highest point of love becasue it is the absolute proof that love is unconditional. In a sense, it is saying to the other person: 'Whatever sort of person you are and whatever you have done to others or to me, I will go on giving to you, for-giving you, and that means loving you.

Often we only love those who love us and are good to us. But the Lord has said: 'That is easy! Everyone does that! But I am asking you to love even your enemies.' In other words, he is asking us to go on giving even to those who do us harm.

But some of you will perhaps object: 'Surely we cannot forgive everything? There are some things that we just cannot overlook!' If you think that, you are very mistaken. Forgiving is not approving what a person has done. It is not refusing to condemn his action. It is refusing to judge the person himself and not enclosing him for ever in his sin.

Others may say: 'Forgiving is submitting to the other person. So it is weakness.' No — it is a sign of strength! Great strength, because love always conquers in the end. Forgiving is the only way to break the circle of hatred and violence. If we fail, it is always because we cannot love to the very end.

Finally, there are those who will murmur

unhappily: 'I would like to forgive and I have tried again and again, but I just cannot.' I can understand them, but I think they are also making a mistake. They are confusing forgiving with forgetting on the one hand and, on the other, forgiving and feeling benevolent or sympathetic towards the person who has harmed them. The Lord certainly does not ask us to do either! It is a question of decision and the will: 'In spite of all my bad memories and even perhaps of feeling deeply repelled by you, I will not judge you, I will go on wishing you well and, if I have the chance, I will do everything I can do to help you to prosper.' As for our own inner peace with regard to that person — it may come later, but perhaps it never will.

Only faith can save us

In the passage from his letter to the Galatians that we have just heard, Saint Paul says: 'What makes a man righteous is not obedience to the Law, but faith in Jesus Christ' (Gal. 2:16) and Jesus told the sinful woman: 'Your faith has saved you!'

What, then, is that faith that saves us? What did that woman believe in? What is so strong that it can wipe out in a moment a whole lifetime of sin and disorder? This is the secret, my friends: the sinful

44

woman believed that, in spite of her sin, she was loved. The Lord never ceases to love us — it is we who fail to love. We are loved by Christ and have always been loved by him. Even before we were created, as Saint Paul says in his letter to the Ephesians, he 'thought of us in his love'. Each of us is a thought of God's love made flesh and Christian faith is first and foremost being sure that, whoever we are and whatever we do, whatever our sin may be, Jesus cannot love us any less, since he loves us and will continue to love us infinitely. Believing, then, is coming close to that love and letting ourselves be created and saved by it.

What kills man is not knowing or believing that he is loved. He is killed when he becomes enclosed within himself and becomes unable to recognise that love because he has placed himself beyond its reach and can no longer be touched by it.

What gives man life on the other hand — life that will never end — is when he believes that love is stronger than anything else, when he opens himself completely to it and becomes strong himself, with the strength of one who knows that he is loved infinitely and unconditionally. That man is already saved. And he will be at peace.

7

*Christmas: a revelation that is a revolution**

I want to ask you a question — are you happy? Well, happy or not, you are doing everything you can to make yourselves happy and also, I hope, those who are not with you today. But I would say straightaway that it is Jesus, the Christmas child, who brings true happiness to man's heart and true peace to the heart of the world. May I suggest that you will understand his extraordinary revelation better and give it a better welcome if you first look at your own little children.

Little children prepare us to receive the message of Christmas

You marvel at the children's happiness when they discover their Christmas presents — the talking doll or the car that runs by remote control. But very soon you are disappointed when they leave their toys in a

*Homily for Christmas Day.

46

corner of the room and begin impatiently to ask when they were going to see their grandparents or their uncle and aunt. Never satisfied, you think, always looking for more presents, new sources of happiness...

But surely you can see what their true happiness is when the feast is over this evening and they come to you to be hugged and kissed before going to bed. You will see it in their eyes. They will tell you then in their own way: 'I am happy because I know you love me. Now I can go to sleep in peace.' What your little children were looking for almost unconsciously in their search for one present after another was, of course, the certainty that they were loved. And what were you looking for, rather clumsily perhaps, by offering them toys and playing, a bit foolishly perhaps, with them? You were telling them: 'I love you.' Is that foolish?

I do not think we can be completely happy, firstly if we are not certain of being loved ourselves, and secondly until we decide to do everything we can to love others. I also think that we shall never be able to achieve that state of loving and being loved on your own. The little child who was born in Bethlehem can show us how to achieve it and how to go further — beyond our wildest dreams.

Being certain of being loved

Firstly, then, being certain of being loved. Saint John tells us that Jesus, the Jewish child from Bethlehem, is 'the true light that enlightens all men . . . coming into the world' (John 1:9), a light that drives out all shadows, fears and doubts from the hearts of those who accept it. That Light is an extraordinary revelation, showing us that the God in whom we believe is not the 'God of the philosophers and scholars', but the God of Love, the God who is our Father.

Christmas is that marvellous declaration of love that God whispers to men in his Son Jesus: 'I love you . . . to the point of death . . . and I will prove it to you . . . with the foolishness of the cross.'

Christmas is the feast of those who welcome that Light and believe they are loved infinitely and unconditionally, because Jesus came to tell them so. That is the heart of God's revelation to us and the heart of faith. That is what can cause a revolution in the lives of those who — like little children in the arms of their parents — believe in the love of their Father 'in heaven', let themselves be loved and created and let themselves be made more fully sons of God every day.

Doing everything we can to love others

Secondly, we can never be truly happy until we decide to do everything we can to love others. And you are among those who try to love others and especially those who suffer most. But you are, of course, often daunted by the immensity of the task! As Martin Luther King said, where are we to find the power to love?

I could reply to that question by quoting great mystics and theologians of the Church, but I will simply say this: If we are enlightened by the Light of Christmas, if we believe we have a Father who is our God and if we believe we all have the same Father — we pray, after all, to 'our' Father — then we are also bound to believe with all our strength that we are all brothers and more closely united by that love than by any blood ties. And if we believe that, how can we allow some of our brothers to die of hunger or to be unemployed, exploited, or unjustly imprisoned or tortured without saying or doing something about it? We are bound to fight surely, but we shall fight out of love for our brothers with Jesus Christ, who entered the arena before we did.

But no struggle for our fellow-men or for justice and peace will ever be completely successful if there are not enough of us in this suffering world to hear our 'Father in heaven' whisper to us: 'It is my son suffering when someone is suffering at your side and that son is your brother. He is one of your family. Go and be with Jesus Christ — he is waiting for you so that he can continue with you to save this world!'

'His own people did not accept him' — why not?

But we have to ask ourselves whether we really trust the child who was born in Bethlehem. Saint John, after all, tells us: 'He came to his own domain and his own people did not accept him' (John 1:11). Why not?

For two thousand years the people of Israel had been expecting a powerful king, but instead a baby came — a baby who was cold and hungry and who cried, a baby who had to leave Egypt because he was being pursued. But they did not recognise him as their Saviour.

And what do we all too frequently expect nowadays? An all-powerful God in the manner of a man! A God who makes us pass exams and find jobs, who cures our illnesses, stops earthquakes and gives bread to everyone — a God who resolves all the problems of society and offers peace to the world.

Yes, we want a powerful God. But the greatness of

the Christmas revelation is that, to our astonishment, we are shown the weakness of God.

Am I really ready to go down on my knees before the child of Bethlehem and call him 'My Lord and my God'? Are we really ready, my dear friends, to believe with the whole of our beings that what is called weakness by men is true strength, because it is the power to love as God loves? We shall, after all, build up a world of peace if we are truly happy and, without neglecting our struggles, strong in the power of Christ's love.

'My own peace I give you, a peace the world cannot give'

Christmas is the festival of peace. But what peace?

Jesus told us: 'My own peace I give you, a peace the world cannot give' (John 14:27), whereas the world tells us: 'Rearm! Have strength in weapons! Frighten your enemies!' And we stand by, impotent and grief-stricken, while our fellow-men on both sides are busy spreading terror.

But Jesus came as a defenceless child to bring a revolution into our lives and we still have not grasped its full meaning. He came to set us free from fear!

Why is it that every normal person is defenceless when he sees a little baby smile? He lays down his arms because he no longer needs them to defend himself. A baby threatens no one. On the contrary, love is born in even the most withered hearts at the sight of a baby smiling. That is surely what Jesus meant when he said: 'Anyone who does not welcome the kingdom of God like a little child will never enter it' (Mark 10:15; Luke 18:17).

So it is only when we have learned to be like little children and rich in love that others will lay down their arms in front of us and become free themselves to love.

Is it very difficult? It is impossible — so long as we do not accept the message of God, who is Love itself and has gone ahead of us to tell us in his Son: 'I love you infinitely. You are my son. Men, you are my brothers.'

8

*Meeting God – and following Him**

For centuries, even before Jesus came among us and in fact probably ever since man has been man, he has been trying to meet God and know him. We are still trying. How shall we succeed? Christ has given us the answer to that question. And it is an answer that upset the ideas and attitudes of men of his own time — and can still upset today.

How can we really know God?

How can we really come to know God? Men have always thought that they could acquire that knowledge by becoming 'learned'. Every ancient religion had its 'initiated', men who had learning and knew and who taught those who did not know. There were many such wise and learned men at the time of Jesus. They were the 'lawyers' and the humble people just followed them.

*Homily for the 14th Sunday in Ordinary Time, Cycle A.

Even now we still very often think we have first to 'study' if we are to meet and know God. How often, for example, have you not heard people say: 'Modern children are learning nothing these days. They do not learn the catechism as we used to! We knew all the answers by heart.' And you yourselves also frequently tell me: 'I would love to bear witness to my faith, but I just do not know enough and cannot answer the questions people put to me.'

Do you have to be very learned? Do you have to have studied before you meet and know God? Jesus Christ seems to reply 'no' to these questions, because he thanked the Father 'for hiding these things from the learned and the clever and revealing them to mere children' (Matt. 11:25). What are we to think of this?

Do we have to be 'simple-minded' to believe?

Is is necessary to be 'simple-minded' in order to believe? No, we have to be simple-hearted. In other words, we have to be open and available, humble and loving.

Man is proud of his intelligence and learning and he is right to be. But this legitimate pride becomes boundless sinful pride and an obstacle to faith when we begin to think we can, with our knowledge conquer not only the world, but also God. Jesus has told us that no one knows the Father except the Son and the ones to whom the Son chooses to reveal him. We can certainly approach God via our reason and we are bound to reflect more and more about our faith. But faith does not come to us as the consequence of reasoning or reflection and it is not simply the sum total of all our knowledge. Man cannot reach God by reason alone. That is not the way to know and love God. God comes to him and reveals himself to him in Jesus Christ. The God of Christians is not a 'God of the philosophers and scholars'! He is a living and loving person. he offers himself to us and we cannot seize hold of him like an object. We can only welcome him as a free gift.

Is the gift of faith for everyone?

Faith is a gift from God. You have all learned that, but have you really understood and accepted it? Many of you must have friends and relatives who are very dear to you, but have 'no faith'. This causes you to suffer and to ask yourselves: Is the gift of faith given to only a few people?' I would like to reassure you. God loves all men infinitely. He reveals himself or he will reveal himself to all men. He makes himself known through the Church, human history, events and people . . . He reveals himself to some of us in time, but, as Scripture tells us, he will reveal himself to others beyond time, when, in the Light, he will say to the man who has served his brothers and expecially the poorest of his fellow-men: 'You did it for me.' In the meantime, man continues to be free both today and tomorrow and he is or will be able to welcome the Lord or to refuse to know him. That is the mystery of love, which, because it is love, cannot force man to love.

Can we hand faith on to others?

That is one anxiety that you have, I know. Another is one that troubles parents especially, when they have done everything possible to hand faith on to their children and then feel they have failed. They question themselves and even blame themselves: 'Have we done everything we ought to have done?' Parents in particular, but also many other Christians accuse themselves of failing to 'convert' their partners in marriage and their friends.

But you cannot 'teach God' to your children, my brothers! You cannot 'show God' to those you love! No one can 'give faith' to his fellow-men. Only God can do that.

Are we condemned to play a passive role, then? No, certainly not! We have the task of 'preparing the ways of the Lord', in other words, of living in such a way that we are ourselves a question for those around us. Looking at us, they will, so long as we do not make the mistake of concealing our faith, ask themselves and perhaps even ask us as Jesus himself did: 'Who is Jesus Christ to you?' Then it will be up to each of us to reply truthfully, from the heart.

Do you say you have done that? But you have not managed to 'convince' anyone? It is not a question of convincing! All you have to do is bear witness. God offers himself and we should not try to force him on anyone.

Putting others on the same road as their brothers

Preparing the ways of the Lord is also putting others on the same road as their brothers. When parents come to me because they are worried about the faith or lack of faith of their grown-up children, I always ask them: 'How have you brought them up to live? Can they go beyond themselves? Can they forget themselves and give themselves to others especially the most vulnerable? Can they commit themselves to fight for their brothers in need? If they can, set your mind at rest. The risen Christ is hidden in the hearts of the poor and the needy. If they can serve them, they will be serving him. And one day they will know him.'

A 'burden' that is light — is that possible?

Let me conclude by saying that knowing God and meeting him in Jesus Christ is good, but it is not enough. What Jesus asks us to do is to follow him. But, you may say, is that not very difficult?

When Jesus was among us, the 'learned and the clever' had made so many rules and regulations that believers were on the point of collapse under the weight of moral and religious laws. It was these people Jesus was talking to when he said: 'Come to me all you who labour and are overburdened and I will give you rest', adding this astonishing statement: 'My yoke is easy and my burden light' (Matt. 11:28-30). But the same Jesus also said on another occasion: 'If anyone wants to be a follower of mine, let him . . . take up his cross and follow me' (Mark 8:34, cf. Matt. 10:37; Luke 9:23; 14:22). These two statements do not, however, contradict each other.

Following Christ is not compelling oneself to observe a great number of trifling regulations of the kind prescribed by the scribes and pharisees. Following Christ is loving. But it is not easy to love because loving means committing oneself to serving one's brothers. And wanting to love and serve others means expecting to bear a heavy burden. So, you may say, following Jesus is very hard.

But here is the secret: No burden is too heavy for the one who loves. The stones carried by the prisoner in a concentration camp weigh the same as those carried by the workman who earns his living in the building trade. But others who carry the same burden of stones, you may ask — fathers who are building up a home for their wives and families — what about them? I would answer: 'Yes, they are carrying the same stones, but they do not weigh the same.'

Following Jesus to build up the kingdom with him is not being condemned to forced labour or even being compelled to perform a 'duty'. It is responding to a love that is offered to us. So we are bound to reply at once: 'Yes, the burden is light!'

9

*Christel confronted with the spirit of evil**

The Gospel of Jesus Christ according to Saint Mark
— 1:2128)

They went as far as Capernaum and as soon as the
sabbath came Jesus went into the synagogue and
began to teach. And his teaching made a deep
impression on them because, unlike the scribes, he
taught them with authority.

In their synagogue just then there was a man
possessed by an unclean spirit and it shouted,
"What do you want with us, Jesus of Nazareth?
Have you come to destroy us? I know who you are:
the Holy One of God." But Jesus said sharply, "Be
quiet! Come out of him!" And the unclean spirit
threw the man into convulsions and with a loud cry
went out of him.

The people were so astonished that they started

*Homily for the 4th Sunday in Ordinary Time, Cycle B.

asking each other what it all meant. "Here is a teaching that is new" they said "and with authority behind it; he gives orders even to unclean spirits and they obey him." And his reputation rapidly spread everywhere, through all the surrounding Galilean countryside.

In this story we have Jesus confronted with evil. But his Word is more powerful and the evil spirit, the 'demon', is overcome and comes out of the man. At the very beginning of his Gospel, then, Mark provides us with a striking example of Jesus' struggle to liberate man completely. This struggle ended in victory and Jesus' sending of his 'Holy Spirit', brought the Kingdom of the Father into being — a new era in which the 'new man', who was 'born again through water and the Spirit' (John 3:5), was to build a 'new world'.

Christ has conquered evil, so have we no further part to play? Of course we have! The spirit of evil is still present in the hearts of men and Jesus and his Spirit are still struggling against it. This continuing struggle is what we have to try to understand today.

Why does God permit evil?
Let us begin with a question: Instead of fighting

against evil, why does God permit it? I imagine every one of you here today has at one time or another heard it said: 'If God existed, evil would not exist!' I remember saying recently in a broadcast that God would not have shown real respect and therefore real love for us if he had handed us a ready-made world and a perfect humanity, with no room for errors, on a plate. Man's greatness and dignity consist in his being able and free to fight with himself so as to build himself up and fight with nature so as to master it, working with knowledge, science and technology until he is able to put nature at the service of his fellow-men.

Just imagine God using the pretext of 'divine goodness' to intervene again and again, telling us, as it were: 'Just stand aside, my son, you will never be able to build up the world and improve the human condition! Sit down and let me get on with the task.' That would be acting paternalistically, not as a father, surely! Confronted with all our mistakes and on the pretext of giving us happiness, he would in this way be depriving us of all responsibility, declaring a 'state of emergency' and concentrating all power in his own hands, thus making himself a dictator and reducing us to the level of puppets.

No, God does not act like this. He will not send a helicopter to the climber who wants to conquer the mountain and take him easily and safely to the top. He will not give employers and workers factories that are already functioning perfectly together with a guarantee that there will be no social and political problems. He will not give the young man, wanting to marry, a beautiful bride who will tell him: 'I cannot do anything else but love you and serve you with complete fidelity.' He will not give parents children already well brought up, who will present them with no problems at all. If he were to behave like that, he would no longer be the God who is Love and we would not be fully human.

As a well-known preacher put it recently, very strikingly, the God in whom we believe is not, as some people seem to think, a God who is all-powerful and domineering, but one who is all-powerful in loving, a prisoner of that Love, risking everything, including his own glory, in his respect for us.

Evil and suffering in the world are the price we pay for our freedom and therefore for our human dignity. We know from experience that if man is deprived of that freedom, on the pretext that he is unable to make proper use of it, he will suffer even more terribly than he suffers in freedom. Man is, after all, not an animal. God made him in an act of love, for love, and therefore wants him to be responsible.

The spirit of evil in man's heart

Man is free, then, and he knows he is free. His greatness consists in that — and also his tragedy, because he takes himself seriously. Because he is made in God's image, he would like to be God. But he is limited. He cannot live alone and can only become fully human in his relationship with other men, just as my hand as part of my body can only be fully hand if it is connected with my wrist, elbow, shoulder, heart and brain... Man, as an unfinished being, is therefore always trying to complete himself by taking hold of the people and things that surround him in order to enrich himself.

We are all in fact 'little gods' and seek to possess things — a house, a car, a television set and so on — for ourselves and, what is much more serious, we seek to possess people. I want my wife or my husband, my children, my friends, all those of whom I am especially fond and I want them for myself. And we say: 'I do not ask anything of anybody! I am quite self-sufficient.'

Well, my little god, my quite self-sufficient person,

64

did you create yourself? Did you build the house you live in? Did you make the television set you watch in the evening? Did you raise the animal whose meat you eat for lunch? Did you write the book you are reading now? Are the people around you really yours? Do they belong to you?

If you receive them, surely it is because they give themselves to you freely. Otherwise you are violating their freedom! I think, my quite self-sufficient friend, you are living on the backs of other people. You are a parasite. You are enclosing yourself within your possessions. You think you possess all those things and people, but in fact you are possessed — by all those evil spirits, those 'demons' which the book of Genesis tells us, have whispered into the heart of man since the beginning this constant temptation: 'Eat the forbidden fruit . . . and you will be like gods.'

Who will deliver us from the spirit of evil?
    Who will drive this evil spirit from our hearts? Who will save us in the depths of our being? Who will set us and our brothers free? Clairvoyants and fortune-tellers? No, they reveal their lack of skill when they blame 'those who cause us evil'. Nor can we either overcome our own pride and selfishness or liberate

mankind from every form of slavery by our own unaided efforts, however justified they may be. We simply do not have enough strength to combat evil on our own. Yet that is something we can hardly bring ourselves to admit! We want to go on struggling alone and for that reason we have to begin the fight again and again. As soon as we think we have at last found freedom — for ourselves and for others — we have to go back once more to the beginning. Why is that? It is because our hearts have not changed.

Jesus is the only one who has conquered evil

Jesus is the only one who is strong enough to transform our 'heart of stone' and give us a 'heart of flesh' (Ezek. 36:26). He is the real 'liberator' who can give us freedom by delivering us from the spirit of evil that so often 'possesses' us and through us builds a world that imprisons and even crushes us.

He does not, however, deliver us by force. He goes through our lives as once he walked on the roads of Palestine, calling on us 'with authority'. His disturbing Word does not, of course, come from his lips of flesh now, but from his Spirit, who whispers into our hearts in concrete situations: 'You should not do that... Give up that way of life...' Through the

Church and our fellow-men, the Spirit invites us again and again to join those who are struggling to build a better world. And, like the possessed man in the synagogue at Capernaum, we shall recognise Jesus one day and the evil spirit in us will resist: 'What do you want with me, Jesus of Nazareth?' . . . I know who you are . . . You have come to destroy me . . . You demand more than I can give: my possessions, my little pleasures, my peace of mind! If I give a little, you ask for more and, if I give more, you ask for everything! Stop tormenting me!'

That is the struggle between the spirit of evil and the Spirit of Christ, a struggle that takes place again and again in our divided lives. It can only end in one way for us: we must welcome the Word of Christ and open ourselves to the Spirit of Love. Then, like the possessed man in th Gospel, we will cry out — the loud cry of freedom!

10

*Jesus sends us**

The Gospel of Jesus Christ according to Saint Mark
— 6:7-13

Jesus made a tour around the villages, teaching.
Then he summoned the twelve and began to send
them out in pairs, giving them authority over the
unclean spirits. And he instructed them to take
nothing for the journey except a staff — no bread,
no haversack, no coppers for their purses. They
were to wear sandals, but, he added, "Do not take a
spare tunic".

And he said to them, "If you enter a house
anywhere, stay there until you leave the district.
And if any place does not welcome you and the
people refuse to listen to you, as you walk away
shake off the dust from under your feet as a sign to
them." So they set off to preach repentance and

*Homily for the 15th Sunday in Ordinary time, Cycle B.

68

they cast out many devils and anointed many sick people with oil and cured them.

Jesus called the twelve, we are told in today's Gospel, and sent them out. It was not just the twelve apostles who were sent on mission. All Jesus' disciples were and still are sent. This call to be a missionary has echoed throughout history in the hearts of every committed Christian. Those of us who have encountered Jesus and known him, if only a little, cannot just look at him and say: 'I love you' and that is all. We are bound to accept that we are sent. Sent, then, but how, to whom and to do what?

Jesus sends us, but how?

The Gospel tells us to take 'no haversack' and 'no coppers for our purses'. Once again, then, Jesus shows himself to be provocative and quite revolutionary. But is what he wants reasonable and, what is more important, can we accept such conditions today?

Let us be honest. Do we not often say to ourselves, even if we lack the courage to say it aloud to others: 'The Gospel is fine, but its teachings cannot be applied literally today. You have to take bits and leave bits.'

Does what the evangelist says mean, for example,

that we should give up all our modern means of proclaiming the good news of Jesus Christ? That we should throw all our books, pamphlets, illustrations and notices into the wastepaper basket? Destroy all our tape recorders and photocopiers? Cancel all our agreements with the broadcasting authorities? Sell all our churches, close all our schools and get rid of all our premises? And there are, after all, so many appeals made by the Church for money to support the missions — should we be deaf to those?

No, like you, I think to do all that would be wrong. But does this view contradict the teaching of the Gospel? I do not think so. God has given us each a head and two arms and we are to use them as well as we can. But we should never forget that we are sent and that the one who sends us has saved the world and set mankind free by dying himself, abandoned and naked, on the cross. He rejected all the 'human' means that were available to him because he wanted to proclaim to the world, not only by what he said, but also by what he did and suffered, that only love can save and set man free.

All our modern human technical means are, in other words, no more than means. Perhaps our greatest temptation today and sometimes our greatest perversion is to believe we can further the kingdom of God by developing and perfecting those means without ensuring a growth in the Love and — I would go as far as to say — the Passion of Christ in the hearts of those who use them. The Church can only be built up by the Holy Spirit acting within us and in what we do.

Jesus sends us, but to whom?

To all men! But we are not to force ourselves on them. What Jesus tells us is: 'If any place does not welcome you and people refuse to listen to you — leave that place!' In other words, do not use pressure and do not recruit members actively. Do not use persuasive or evocative advertising methods that will virtually force people to join the Church!

We are sent into the world, but not as sales representatives urging people to buy goods with miraculous properties or as insurance agents selling all risks policies. Our task is not to persuade workers to join multinational commercial enterprise. We are the disciples of a living person whom we want our brothers to get to know.

Of course, we have to live the Gospel before proclaiming it and to commit ourselves to following

Christ in order to build up the kingdom of God. But we also have to do something that we have all too often neglected to do in the past — we have to name Jesus when we speak to our brothers. We have to say to them, for example: 'As Christians, we are not working alone. We have a friend who is much greater than we are and we would like you to meet him as well. We will introduce him to you and then, when we have done that, we will quietly retire into the background and let you get to know him more intimately on your own.'

Just think how often you suffer, those of you who are parents or teachers or who are active in various movements, because you feel unable to hand faith on to the people you meet. You are not trying to 'teach' them a 'religion' or a code of morality, you know that, of course, but want to help them to get to know a person, Jesus Christ.

You should remember, however, that you will never succeed in getting your fellow-men to become Christians yourself. Christ is freely chosen and freely followed! Does that mean we should give up all attempts to discuss or explain faith? No, I think not. But it does mean giving up using all available means to draw others in. Remember again what Jesus himself said: 'If any place does not welcome you and people refuse to listen to you — leave that place!' But remember too the astonishing words that he added to that instruction: we are to go away 'as a sign to them'. So our leaving is a sign, by which we bear witness to the fact that, like Jesus himself, we respect our brothers' essential freedom and show that our love for them is authentic.

Jesus sends us, but to do what?

According to Saint Mark, we are sent 'to preach repentance', in other words, to tell people that their attitudes must change, that they must lead different lives and follow a new way.

But I have the impression that nowadays our task is not so much to follow a new way as to find a way at all. Many young people — and many older ones too — simply do not know where they are going. They have lost all sense of direction. One has only to listen to the questions that are being asked all around one, urgent and often very distressed questions: Why am I studying? Why should I work? Why have a family? Why bring children into the world? Why suffer? Why should I grow old? What is the purpose of living? What is the meaning of my life? Of life as a whole? Of death? Has man any significance? Or the universe or history? Or is it ultimately just absurd?

Revealing the meaning of life to the world

We Christians must try to answer these questions our brothers are asking. And we know what the answer is, because Jesus Christ has given it to us and Saint Paul has expressed it beautifully at the beginning of his Letter to the Ephesians: 'Blessed be God the Father of our Lord Jesus Christ . . . Before the world was made' — and why was the world made? — 'he chose us, chose us in Christ, to be holy and spotless and to live through love in his presence, determining that we should become his adopted sons through Jesus Christ' (Eph. 1:3-4).

So we are not just hanging in a vacuum, with no origin and no destiny. Our life has direction and meaning. We do not have a before and an afterwards, but an infinity — an infinity of uncreated Love. The direction and significance of our life and that of the whole world is that we are going from eternal Love to eternal Love. What distinguishes us from flowers or animals is that we are able to know that Love and open ourselves to it. That is because Love has a face — the face of Jesus of Nazareth. He said of himself: 'I am

74

the Way' and 'Whoever lives and believes in me will never die' (John 14:6; 11:26).

Faith, then, is believing in that love and letting oneself be loved. Prayer is putting oneself consciously in the orbit of that Love and being created and saved by it. Building up the kingdom of God is opening oneself to that Love and, strengthened by its infinite energy, working to build up a free and just brotherhood of man.

That is the meaning of life and the direction it should take. The goal is also described by Saint Paul: 'to bring everything together under Christ as head, everything in the heavens and everything on earth' (Eph. 1:10).

Today Jesus sends us, without any luggage and with only our own lives to offer, to our brothers who so often go astray on ways that lead nowhere. Let us, then, overcome our reticence and fears and speak out. If we really believe and live what we believe, we should be glad to offer to all men of good will the Way of Jesus of Nazareth!

11

Lord, tell us: which camp are you in[*]

A Reading from the book of Numbers — 11:24-29

Moses gathered seventy elders of the people and brought them around the Tent. The Lord came down in the cloud. He spoke with him, but took some of the Spirit that was on him and put it on the seventy elders. When the Spirit came on them they prophesied, but not again.

Two men had stayed back in the camp; one was called Eldad and the other Medad. The Spirit came down on them; though they had not gone to the Tent, their names were enrolled among the rest. These began to prophesy in the camp. The young man ran to tell this to Moses. "Look," he said "Eldad and Medad are prophesying in the camp." Then Joshua, the son of Nun, who had served Moses from his youth, said, "My Lord Moses, stop them!" Moses answered him, "Are you jealous on

[*]Homily for the 26th Sunday in Ordinary Time. Cycle B.

my account? If only the whole people of the Lord were prophets and the Lord gave his Spirit to them all!" Then Moses went back to the camp, the elders of Israel with him.

The Gospel of Jesus Christ according to Saint Mark — 9:38-40

John said to him, "Master, we saw a man who is not one of us casting out devils in your name and because he was not one of us we tried to stop him". But Jesus said, "You must not stop him; no one who works a miracle in my name is likely to speak evil of me. Anyone who is not against us is for us."

Men, both individually and collectively, are often very good at drawing dividing lines that cannot be crossed. At saying: 'On this side is good, on that side is evil. Truth is on this side and error is on the other. Heaven is here, hell is there.'

That is bad enough, but even worse is when God is claimed for one camp or the other: God is with us! How often that has happened in history! Two armies are drawn up against each other, ready to fight to the death and the soldiers on each side claim the same God for themselves and call on him to support them in their just war. Surely we ought to go to God himself and find out what he thinks!

They do not belong to our camp!

I believe he will tell us what our attitude should be through the Old Testament and the Gospel readings for today. In the Book of Numbers, Moses, we are told, has withdrawn to pray with the seventy elders of the people. The Spirit of God has come down on them and they have begun to prophesy. And then a young man goes to warn Moses that two other elders who had not joined the others were also prophesying and should be stopped. But Moses' reply is unexpected: 'Are you jealous on my account? If only the whole people were prophets and the Lord gave his Spirit to them all!'

The second text is from Mark's Gospel. Here one of the apostles reacts violently to a similar situation: 'Master, we saw a man who is not one of us casting out devils in your name and because he was not one of us we tried to stop him.' But Jesus replies: 'You must not stop him! . . . Anyone who is not against us is for us.'

'The Spirit blows wherever he pleases'

Let us be honest — these reactions do not surprise

us very much. We may even be quite used to them. We quote from the Bible and say — and believe — 'the Spirit blows wherever he pleases'. We are also very glad that the Second Vatican Council taught that the Spirit of Jesus goes far beyond the frontiers of the Church! But... do we not behave sometimes as though only we possessed the truth? As though others did not share it at all?

I could go further! We Christians have left our ghettoes, in other words, the Christian communities in which we hold, quite legitimately, our meetings. We work side by side now with all men of good will to build up a better world. But are we really ready to accept that those we work with are as good as, and even better than us? Or do we only grudgingly put up with them and search desperately for arguments to convince them of our superiority? Do we think, perhaps: 'Yes, they do good. They are very efficient. But their achievement is not quite the same as ours, because we work with God. They work on their own.'

If so, then I think the Lord is saying to us what he said through Moses: 'Do not be jealous!' He might even go on: 'Rather be glad, for I am with them as I am with you!'

The Lord, my brothers, is not in our camp or in theirs! He is everywhere. Christ is not just with one particular man or one kind of man — he is with all men.

The dividing line goes through the heart of every man

At the same time, however, I am bound to say there are times when the Spirit of Christ is active and times when he is not, times when the kingdom of the Father is growing and times when it is not. There are dividing lines. There are iron curtains — and also curtains of gold, of ideas and of flesh! There are all kinds of frontiers, but they are not where we erect them. They do not exist between certain people or certain groups of people. They go through the heart of every man in the world.

Christ is present with everyone who really loves. He is only absent from those who do not love. Saint John states this categorically: 'Love comes from God... Anyone who fails to love can never have known God... Anyone who claims to be in the light but hates his brother is still in the dark. But anyone who loves his brother is living in the light' (1 John 4:7-8; 2:9-10). And Jesus himself tells us in the Gospel of the Last Judgment that all men will be judged on the basis of their attitude towards others and especially towards the poor and the 'least of the brothers', saying that

80

'insofar as you did it to one of them, you did it to me' (see Matt 25:40).

Is there any difference, then, between Christians and non-Christians?

I know what you are going to ask now, my friends. It is a worrying question, because we are all a bit like the stay-at-home son in the parable, trying to be faithful, and disturbed when our prodigal brother is regarded as better than us. Then there are the labourers hired at the eleventh hour to work in the vineyard and paid as much as us, who 'have done a heavy day's work in all the heat' (Matt 20:12). It is not easy for us to accept that all those guests who have not been invited to the feast may be the first to sit down at the Lord's table tomorrow. In other words, we are bound to ask ourselves: 'Why should we be Christians? Why try to follow Jesus Christ in this life if those who do not know him are as good as we are and perhaps even better and may enter the kingdom of God before we do?' And the inevitable conclusion is: 'It is unjust! There must be a difference.'

You are right, there is a difference, but it is not to be found where we so often think it is! Let me illustrate what I mean with an image.

A blind gardener appeared recently on the television. I forget which channel. All I remember is that I was very impressed. I watched him sowing, planting and caring for the plants as they grew. We were not told whether his flowers and vegetables were better or less good than those of gardeners who could see. The only difference between him and the others — a terrible difference, to be sure — was that the blind gardener worked in complete darkness.

We Christians can see

We are Christians and we can see! What does our faith give us? It gives us sight. Faith enables us to see through Jesus of Nazareth, the Son of the living God. Faith also enables us to see, in the heart of the world, the Spirit of the risen Jesus mysteriously at work among men — all men — for the building up of the kingdom of his Father. Faith also enables us to see through the acts that the Church gives us, the sacraments, Jesus himself, continuing to offer himself to those who know him. And since we are unfortunately not always able to see well, often because we are looking too closely at the ground, faith also enables us to trust in the Church, our watchful mother, who tells us: 'The Spirit of Jesus cannot be present just now, because this attitude — or this way of thinking — cannot lead to man's full growth and cannot further justice, peace or love in the world.'

We are Christians working in the Father's garden and we can see. Do we have a greater degree of responsibility, then? Yes, in a sense we do, but every man, whoever he may be, is also responsible for his own life and for that of his brothers. The real difference between the man who does not believe and us who do is that we see the one who is working with us and, because we see him and believe in him, the risen Christ who has conquered sin and death, we cannot lose heart and we are and must always be happy and at peace.

Bearing witness to the Light

In this world where we as Christians feel more and more isolated and where we have to work among those who are blind or do not see well, we should bear witness by our hope and joy to the Light. Jesus himself has told us: 'You are the light of the world' (Matt 5:14). One day perhaps many of the blind gardeners will be healed and be able to see, beyond the flowers and vegetables they cultivate together with us, the one who makes all things grow.

12

*What is the use of praying**

The Gospel of Jesus Christ according to Saint Luke —
18:1-8

Jesus told them a parable about the need to pray
continually and never lose heart.

"There was a judge in a certain town" he said
"who had neither fear of God nor respect for man.
In the same town there was a widow who kept on
coming to him and saying, 'I want justice from you
against my enemy!' For a long time he refused, but
at last he said to himself, 'Maybe I have neither fear
of God nor respect for man, but since she keeps on
pestering me I must give this widow her just rights,
or she will persist in coming and worry me to
death.'"

And the Lord said, "You notice what the unjust
judge has to say? Now will not God see justice done
to his chosen who cry to him day and night even
when he delays to help them? I promise you, he will
see justice done to them and done speedily. But

*Homily for the 22nd Sunday in Ordinary Time, Cycle C.

when the Son of Man comes, will he find any faith on earth?''

Saint Luke's aim is very obvious — he tells us himself that Jesus told this parable of the unjust judge to show his disciples 'the need to pray constantly and never lose heart'. And Jesus tells us again and again that no one who prays ever prays in vain: prayer is always effective. Let me give you just two examples. According to Matthew, 'Ask and it will be given to you; search and you will find; knock and the door will be opened to you' (Matt 7:7). And in the fourth Gospel, 'You may ask what you will and you shall get it' (John 15:7). In this parable, he goes even further, advising his disciples to insist like the importunate widow in her claim for justice. If we are insistent, he says, God will let himself be persuaded because he is our loving Father.

But millions of people pray and are not heard

'But,' you will object, 'in my experience that is just not true. I have often prayed and have not been heard!' And surely we have all at one time or another been disturbed and even deeply upset by God's apparent indifference and silence in the presence of terrible human suffering.

How many millions of mothers — to take one particularly tragic example — could testify to the fact that they have pleaded and pleaded with God to cure their

85

child of a fatal illness or at least to lessen the suffering and, in the nineteen-forties for example, not to let him die in a concentration camp or on the field of battle in a 'just' war.

And how many of those mothers could also testify that they prayed in vain! Some of them may of course have made votive offerings in thanksgiving to God for having spared their son — because the bullet did not strike him, but another mother's son fighting at his side. But these prayers of thanksgiving must surely be far fewer than the tears shed by millions whose prayer was apparently not heard.

What we have, in other words, is the terrible problem of a God who is our Father, but who seems to want to protect some children more than others. Is it blasphemous to express this problem in this way? Does it point to a lack of faith? No, it does not.

Jesus' own prayer was not heard

Let us consider the case of another man who was confronted long before we were with God's terrifying silence in the presence of prayer. That man was Jesus of Nazareth.

One evening, in 'sadness' and 'great distress', because he had, from the human point of view, completely failed in his mission, and overcome by 'sudden fear', anticipating inevitable torture and death, he pleaded with his Father to deliver him: 'My Father, if it is possible, let this cup pass me by!' (Matt 26:37-9; Mark 14:33-6; Luke 22:41-2). But his Father remained deaf to his prayer!

I know what you are thinking, because you are all 'orthodox' Christians: 'But surely Jesus added: "Nevertheless, let your will be done, not mine"!' that is true, of course, but it is also true that a few hours later, on the cross, he also cried out from the cross: 'My God, my God, why have you deserted me?' (Matt 27:46; Mark 15:34).

That is the cry that we have heard echoing throughout history — a great uninterrupted cry going up to God from millions of men and women suffering on their crosses: 'God, our God, why do you desert us? Why do you let innocent people suffer and die? Are you insensitive? Are you deaf? Yet you are called our Father and we your sons!'

Why does God remain silent?

This bring us into contact with the very heart of the mystery of God. Let us try in all humility to understand it.

Was it God's 'will' that Jesus should suffer and die? No, it was not. No father wants his innocent son to die, God the Father least of all. But no loving father can prevent his son from carrying out the mission that has

87

been entrusted to him and from offering himself freely and in love in order to save his brothers. If he were to prevent that offering, he would not be respecting his son's freedom and would therefore not be authentically loving him.

So, because of his love for his son Jesus and for us, also his sons, God simply could not intervene to prevent Jesus from suffering and dying. We are bound to use inadequate human words to express ourselves and so we may say: he had to stand 'impotently' by while Jesus, the Saviour of his brothers, suffered and died on the cross.

God's silence in the presence of Jesus on the cross explains his silence in the presence of crucified humanity

Contemplating the mystery of Christ suffering and dying on the cross leads us on to consider God's silence in the presence of crucified humanity!

If we were honest we would all admit that we have often longed to have and believe in a god who worked miracles and intervened in our lives to settle our insoluble problems and deliver us from our sufferings and the crosses that we put on one another's backs by failing to love one another.

But believing in that kind of god is not believing in the true God. The God who loves us and whom we love has given us, both individually and collectively, the task of completing man, 'made in his image and likeness', in other words, of completing humanity and transforming the world and putting it at the service of our brothers. He does not want to take our place and will not intervene, at least directly, even if we harm ourselves seriously and even if we kill each other. He respects our freedom and trusts us. That is the marvelous proof of his infinite love for and of our greatness as men.

We, then, have to make the grain of wheat grow and share the bread with all our brothers, build houses, factories and town and provide work for all men, create justice in society and peace between the nations, fight with all our strength against suffering and disease and not just bring children into the world, but also bring them up well.

Let us, then, not ask God to take our place! We may pray to him and plead with him, but if our prayer is not admissible, he will not answer it!

Why pray then? And how is prayer effective?

God can certainly perform 'miracles'. That is clear from the Gospel. But they are undoubtedly exceptional and they are always the 'sign' of another gift. Just think of the many physical healings, which are signs of healings from sin and of the miracle of the loaves and the marriage feast at Cana, both signs of the Eucharist.

Generally speaking, however, despite our prayers,

God does not work miracles in our lives, in the sense of changing the course of the laws of nature or suspending them. But he does always hear and answer our prayer at another level.

If we believe in him, he gives us the infinite power of his Love and it is faith in that Love that can enable us to 'move mountains', as Jesus himself put it. In other words, we shall be able to fight against evil and to bear suffering and offer it, with him, for the salvation of the world.

That is why it is not wrong to say that prayer is effective and that no one who prays ever prays in vain, since God cannot refuse that Love to anyone who asks him for it. But for God's sake let us not behave childishly in God's presence! I mean, of course, let us not ask him to take our place and do 'our' will: 'Our Father, let "my" will be done.' Let us behave rather like true children, believing with all our heart in his infinite Love, even though he is apparently silent and seems not to answer our prayer.

Praying is coming close to God and opening ourselves to his will, not ours. And it is his will that we should complete the work of his creation — man, humanity and the world — with all the means at our disposal, struggling, but with the infinite power of his saving Love. For we shall never be victorious in that struggle if it is not, with Jesus Christ, a struggle of Love.